Introduc

G **ower**, lying to the west of Swansea, ∖ Natural Beauty' (AONB) in Britain. ∕ is a compact area that holds a surprisin the coast and inland. There are three N; Bay, Gower Coast and Whiteford Burro∖ local reserves, owned by wildlife trusts, the National conservation organisations. Information on some nature reserves can be found at www.the-gower.com/naturereserves/nature. Although generally low-lying, Gower has a number of areas of open access hill land and is the location of two long-distance walking routes – the Gower Coast Path and the Gower Way, sections of which feature in this guide.

Coastal scenery – beaches and cliff top paths – features strongly in this guide, with several of Gower's Nature Reserves (including all three National Reserves) being located on the coast. The coastline varies considerably, with rocky limestone cliffs, outcrops and small beaches to the south; the long sandy beaches of Rhossili and Whiteford to the west; the salt marshes and tidal flats of the Burry Inlet and River Loughor to the north.

The hills of the peninsula, as well as offering a range of great views, pass prehistoric sites, holy and other wells (the underlying limestone gives rise to many springs), church and castle sites, as well as local nature reserves. Riverside and woodland walks lead into some of the more secluded parts of the area, taking in other local nature reserves and passing in sight of cave entrances as well as further historic and prehistoric features of interest. A number of walks centre around the Gower Heritage Centre at Parkmill, near the middle of Gower AONB.

The individual walks are mostly easy or moderate in type, with the majority quite short in length, although many can be combined into longer routes. This guide can also be used as a basis for planning linear routes, making use of the Gower Explorer and other bus services. All walks are accessible by bus, with timetables available from Swansea's Quadrant Bus Station, various Swansea and Gower Area Tourist Information Centres or at www.swansea.gov.uk/transport.

The use of walking boots and suitable clothing are recommended. Walkers are advised to check weather forecasts, the times of high tides if following beach routes and to check on-site safety notices. Exercise caution if you wish to detour from the routes in this book to visit such places as Worm's Head, Burry Holms or the Old Lighthouse at Whiteford Point. The location of each walk is shown on the back cover, together with estimated walking times and other details inside the covers.

Please follow The Country Code – and enjoy your walking!

MUMBLES HILL

DESCRIPTION An easy walk of about 1½ miles, with one main ascent. The hill is a local nature reserve, the upper levels being limestone grassland, with heathland on the lower slopes. Paths running around the crest of the hill provide excellent views towards Mumbles pier and lighthouse and also over Swansea Bay. With information boards, a viewpoint and plenty of benches, the hill also has the remains of World War II gun platforms and bunkers. Allow about 1 hour for the walk.

START Car Park, SS 627872.

PUBLIC TRANSPORT Bus no. 2B from/to Swansea stops a short distance from start of walk.

From the car park, head for the road and turn RIGHT. (If arriving by bus, alight at the roadside bus stop. Head back along the bus route for a few yards to the waymarked track leading uphill on the right). Follow the pavement until reaching a waymarked track leading up the hill on the left. Cross the road with care and follow the track uphill, soon coming to a Mumbles Hill Local Nature Reserve Information Board. Continue to follow the track until nearing the crest of the hill.

2 At this point, use the network of paths leading off to the right, which provide views over the pier, lighthouse and sea. Gradually follow paths round to the left, towards the mast on the hilltop. Continue beyond the mast to reach the viewpoint, where there is a second information board and picnic benches.

3 Continue along a path leading alongside the railings to reach the trig point. Follow the waymarked path to the 'Bunkers and Guns' ignoring other paths leading to Mumbles Village and to Thistleboon. When ready, return on the outward route past the trig point to the viewpoint and benches (other paths that lead back towards the viewpoint are overgrown at time of writing). Turn RIGHT and follow the track back down the hill to the road.

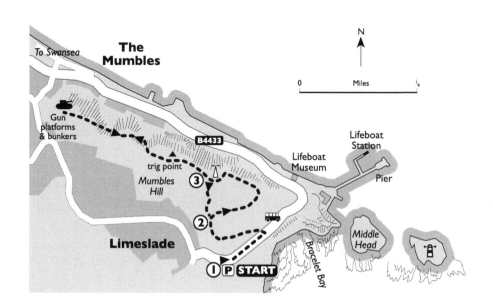

WALK 2

BISHOPS WOOD, ST PETER'S WELL & CASWELL BAY

DESCRIPTION A moderate walk, of about 1¾ miles, around a local nature reserve, passing through deciduous woodland and visiting an attractive modern roundhouse (with picnic benches). A short there-and-back-again section of the route leads to the remains of St Peter's Chapel and Well. Nearby Caswell Bay is sandy at low tide and has refreshment facilities. Allow about 1¼ hours for the walk.

START Caswell Bay car park, SS 596877.

PUBLIC TRANSPORT Bus no. 2B from/to Swansea (Summer only) stops near car park.

1 Head towards the back of the car park to reach an information point about Bishops Wood Local Nature Reserve. When ready, join the path to the left of the information point. After a few yards, bear LEFT towards the red-topped Beech Trail waymark post. Follow winding steps and rustic waymark posts uphill and then to the right, along the top edge of the wood. When the fence on the left begins to descend, head downhill (steps part of the way).

2 Towards the bottom of the hill look for narrow gaps in the two fences on the left. Go through the first gap (but not the second) and immediately turn LEFT along a sunken bridleway. Follow this up a rise, passing open land on the right. Look for a narrow gap in the fence on the right, with a path beyond leading towards the chapel arch. The remains of the well can be seen on the left, a few yards further on. When ready, retrace the outward route down the track to the gap in the two fences. Go back through the gap in the fence on the right and head HALF LEFT to reach the roundhouse.

3 Go through the roundhouse and immediately bear LEFT and go through a small gate. Head LEFT for a short way and then pass through a narrow gap in a fence on the right. Follow the waymarked path up an open slope to a waymark post and bench. Turn RIGHT and follow a path indicated by rustic waymark posts and red/white signs. Shortly after coming in sight of a house off to the left, take the right fork in the path. Follow the path downhill, returning to the car park near the nature reserve information point.

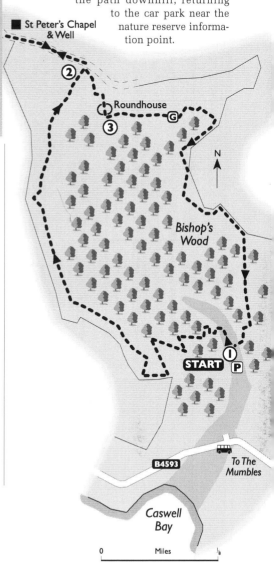

3

RAMS TOR, ROTHERS TORR & NEWTON CLIFF

DESCRIPTION A moderate 6 mile walk, using paths along cliffs with excellent views out to sea and over rocky inlets. The cliffs are open access land, from which seasonal bird migrations can be observed. Caswell Bay is at the mid-point of the walk and has refreshment facilities. Allow about 4 hours for the walk.
START Car Park near Limeslade, SS 627872 .
PUBLIC TRANSPORT Bus no. 2B from/to Swansea stops a short distance from car park

the left, passing houses and then beach huts.
• **Low Tide Option** Descend steps to the beach. Head RIGHT on this and rejoin the High Tide Option via steps at the far end of Langland Bay.

4 Follow the path (a mixture of tarmac, concrete and unsurfaced) along the cliff tops to reach Caswell Bay. Ignore a waymark post on the right about three-quarters of the way along this section of the walk.

5 When ready, retrace the outward route as far as the waymark post passed in stage 4. Leave the main path and bear LEFT up the steps. Follow the path up to the top of the hill. At the waymark post turn LEFT and follow the edge of the golf course to the next waymark post. Turn RIGHT here and cross the golf course with care towards a further waymark post near an abandoned house.

1 From the car park (if arriving by bus, alight near entrance to car park), head for the road and turn LEFT. Follow the pavement to the junction with a road on the right coming down from Thistleboon (make a detour to visit Limeslade Bay if you wish, afterwards returning to the road by the junction). Cross the road with care and go up the waymarked steps to the left of the junction, next to a café.

2 At the top of the ascent follow the path round to the left and along the high ground. Ignore paths leading off to the right and keep AHEAD. At a four-way waymark post, also continue AHEAD. Eventually follow the path downhill to join a tarmac path. Turn RIGHT and follow the tarmac path to Langland Bay.

3 On reaching Rothers Torr beach (by the café) there are: • **High Tide Option** Stay on the tarmac path as this curves round to

6 Follow the path to the right of the house, bearing LEFT at the next waymark post. Continue to follow the route indicated by two waymark posts. On reaching a fork in the track, follow the left fork for some yards towards a waymark post on the right.

7 Follow the track between houses and continue AHEAD on the concrete surface. On nearing tarmac, bear RIGHT down steps and follow the next two waymark signs. Join a path running along the edge of the golf course, between trees and a fence. At the end of the fence, cross the golf course with care, heading towards a waymark post near the buildings.

8 Follow the path to the left and then turn LEFT on a lane. Follow the lane down towards Langland Bay, looking out for a turning on the right leading down to the beach. Retrace the outward route either along the tarmac path or across the beach to Rothers Torr. Head back towards the start of the walk, remaining on the lower, tarmac, path (way-marked as Gower Coast Path) throughout. On reaching a road, follow this back past the Limeslade Bay area to the car park.

WALK 4

CASWELL BAY, BRANDY COVE & PWLLDU BAY

DESCRIPTION Starting from Caswell Bay, this 4½ mile moderate walk starts with a beach section for which low tide is advisable. The route heads towards Brandy Cove (used for smuggling during the Napoleonic Wars). From here, the walk continues up through woods to follow a cliff top route to Pwlldu Bay. The Gower Coast Path, further down the cliffs, is used to return to Brandy Cove, from where an inland path and road lead back to Caswell Bay. Allow 2¾ hours.
START Caswell Bay car park, SS 596877.
PUBLIC TRANSPORT Bus no. 2B from/to Swansea (Summer only) stops near car park

follow the path up through woodland to a third stile.

3 Continue AHEAD for a short way and, on reaching an unmarked wooden post, turn RIGHT. Follow the path along the hill, ignoring a gate on the right. Cross an unmarked stile and bear LEFT on the track beyond. Follow the track downhill and then round to the left towards Pwlldu Bay. Cross a footbridge and follow the track round to the left, past houses, to the beach.

4 When ready, head inland from the bay, across a shingle bank. On nearing the stream turn LEFT and head back towards the

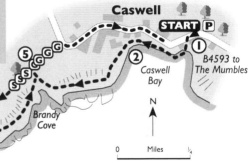

I From the car park, cross the road with care to Caswell Bay. Head RIGHT along Caswell Bay beach. Pass the coastguard buildings, at the top of a shingle bank off to the right. Head HALF RIGHT to reach a way-marked path in an angle of the bay.

2 Go up the steps and follow the path round to the left. Continue along the path to reach a junction of routes above Brandy Cove. Descend to cove if wished, returning to the junction when ready and following the track leading inland. Before reaching a waymarked gate, cross a stile on the left. Cross the field to a second stile and

houses. On reaching the track, turn RIGHT and follow this over the footbridge. Follow the track back up the hill, in the direction of Brandy Cove. Ignore a footpath sign leading off to the left. On reaching the Coast Path sign, bear RIGHT and follow the Coast Path back to Brandy Cove.

5 On reaching Brandy Cove, turn LEFT and follow the track up the valley. Go through a waymarked gate and turn RIGHT up the steps. Go through another gate and follow the path along the right hand side of the field. Go through a gate and follow the track AHEAD. When the track turns right, continue AHEAD on a path to a kissing gate and road. Turn RIGHT and follow the road down to Caswell Bay.

WALK 5

BISHOPSTON VALLEY, PWLLDU BAY & BRANDY COVE

DESCRIPTION An energetic 5¼ mile walk (some ascents/descents but also uneven ground in places – walking boots are essential), leading down from the village of Kittle into National Trust owned woodland. Paths and bridleways lead down through the wood, alongside a stream for a good part of the way, to reach Pwlldu Bay. From here, a track across the cliff tops provides a contrast in scenery, descending through further woodland to Brandy Cove. A track and lane passing Swansea Community Tree Nursery Project (01792 361763 or www.coedenfach.org.uk for details of opening times), leads to Pyle (Post Office/shop) before returning by lane and footpath to Bishopston Valley. The return route through the wood makes use of a dry streambed and passes near three caves, the latter two are especially of interest

START Roadside parking on B4436 in Kittle, SS 574893.

PUBLIC TRANSPORT Bus no. 14, between Swansea and Pennard Cliffs, passes through Kittle.

I Start on the the B4436 opposite the Beaufort Arms Hotel. Cross the small green and follow a track leading ahead, soon passing a National Trust Plinth and a bench, both on the left. On reaching Great Kittle Farm, leave the main track for a path running to the left of the boundary fence and continuing ahead into Bishopston Valley woods. When the path divides, take the right fork. Follow the path up steps and past an outcrop on the right, where there is a view over the valley. Follow the path down steps and then back up further steps. Pass through a more open stretch of ground, with fields visible to the right. Follow the path back into the wood and descend – steeply in places – to reach the junction with a bridleway.

2 Turn RIGHT and follow the bridleway, with a stream to the left, to reach a footbridge. Do not cross the footbridge, but continue to follow the track alongside the stream, in the direction of Pwlldu. On sighting old drystone walling, keep to the left of this. On reaching an open field, follow the track along the left hand side of this to reach a second footbridge, with a waymark sign for Pwlldu. Again, do not cross the footbridge, but continue towards Pwlldu, bearing HALF LEFT at the next two junctions of track, with the stream not far away to the left.

3 On reaching a three-way waymark post, take the path leading HALF LEFT for Pwlldu. Descend a zigzag path by means of steps and turn RIGHT on a track at the bottom. Pass another National Trust Plinth and descend HALF LEFT towards a footbridge. Do not cross the footbridge, but turn RIGHT and follow the track past the houses to Pwlldu Bay. When ready, head inland across the shingle bank. On reaching the stream, turn LEFT and head back to the track. Turn RIGHT and go over the footbridge.

4 Follow the main track round to the right and uphill, ignoring footpath signs on the left and a coast path sign on the right. On reaching a stile on the right, cross this and follow the path AHEAD. Ignore a gate on the left and continue AHEAD and then round to the left. On reaching an unmarked wooden post, on the right, turn LEFT. Cross a stile and follow a path, with steps, down through the wood to a second stile. Cross the field to a third stile. Cross and head LEFT to a waymarked gate and track through the wood. At a waymark post, continue AHEAD. Go through a gate, near Hareslade Farm.

5 Continue AHEAD on the farm access track. On this section of the walk, Swansea Community Tree Nursery Project (see description above) will be seen off to the left. Join a tarmac lane and continue AHEAD. Ignore footpath sign on the left and continue AHEAD to the junction, with the Post Office on the left. Turn LEFT and follow the lane, continuing AHEAD at a junction by a waymark post. Pass a driveway entrance

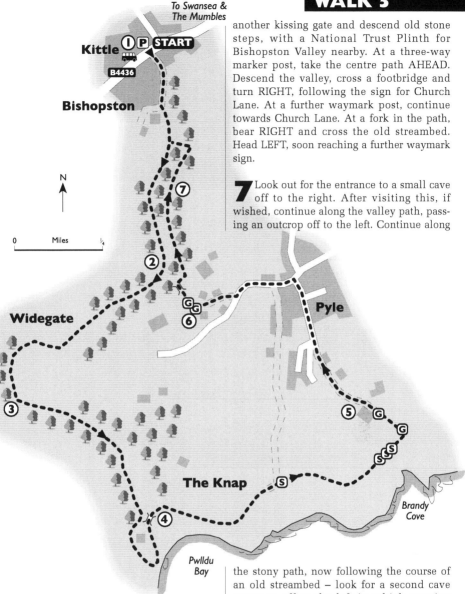

another kissing gate and descend old stone steps, with a National Trust Plinth for Bishopston Valley nearby. At a three-way marker post, take the centre path AHEAD. Descend the valley, cross a footbridge and turn RIGHT, following the sign for Church Lane. At a further waymark post, continue towards Church Lane. At a fork in the path, bear RIGHT and cross the old streambed. Head LEFT, soon reaching a further waymark sign.

7 Look out for the entrance to a small cave off to the right. After visiting this, if wished, continue along the valley path, passing an outcrop off to the left. Continue along the stony path, now following the course of an old streambed – look for a second cave entrance off to the left in which running water can be heard. On sighting a waymark post, on the left, cross the old streambed and follow the path up steps towards Kittle. Pass a third, fenced off, cave on the left. On reaching the junction with another path, turn RIGHT. Follow the path back past Great Kittle Farm and continue along the access track back to the village.

on the right and very soon take a track leading HALF RIGHT. When the track meets a concrete surface, look for a kissing gate on the left.

6 Go through the kissing gate and follow the path along the right hand side of the field, soon between fences. Go through

EAST CLIFFS, PWLLDU BAY, BISHOPSTON & LOCKWAY WOODS

DESCRIPTION Starting with a walk along East Cliffs to Pwlldu Head (with plenty of great views on the way), this 4¼ mile route then crosses a short stretch of farmland and descends via an old trackway to the shingle beach at Pwlldu Bay. Heading back inland, the walk then crosses another three fields, before entering the National Trust owned Bishopston Woods. A bridleway leads through these, before turning south to return to Pennard Cliffs by track and then lane. Allow about 2¼ hours.
START Car Park at Pennard Cliffs, SS 555874.
PUBLIC TRANSPORT Bus no. 14 from/to Swansea stops adjacent to car park.

1 From the car park/bus stop, head seaward to reach National Trust Information board and waymark signs. Bear LEFT, following the coastal path waymark signs. Walk roughly parallel to the cliffs – there are a considerable number of paths to choose from in this open access area.

2 After about 1¼ miles, ascend to Pwlldu Head, from where there are views towards Caswell Bay. From this point, follow the footpath downhill and then re-ascend to reach a waymarked gate into farmland. Go through the gate and follow the path running to the right of the fence. Go through a second waymarked gate and head across the field to a further gate. Follow the path through a mixture of scrub and woodland, passing through a gap in a fence. At a waymark sign, bear HALF LEFT to pass through a gate. Continue AHEAD for a short way to a track.

3 Turn RIGHT and follow the track downhill. On nearing a gate leading to a house, turn SHARP RIGHT onto a bridleway. Follow this sunken and then winding track downhill. On reaching the junction with another track, turn RIGHT and follow the track past houses to reach Pwlldu Bay. When ready, head inland from the bay to reach a track near the Bishopston Pill (stream/small river).

4 Turn LEFT and follow the track back towards the houses. On reaching the junction with the bridleway, turn RIGHT and retrace the outward route back up the hill. On reaching the junction near the gate to the first house, cross the track to the waymarked footpath opposite. Cross a stile and follow the path alongside the boundary fence to a second stile. Continue AHEAD on a path running to the left of a new hedge and cross a third stile. Head for the right hand side of the field and follow this for some way, until reaching a stile into woodland, just to the left of a gate.

5 Enter the woodland and ignore the path leading left, alongside the fence. Continue into the woodland, passing the remains of an old stile and steps. Follow a path leading downhill and to the left. Cross a fallen tree trunk, by means of naturally occurring steps, and continue along the path to reach a waymarked junction.

6 Take the path leading ahead, signposted for Kittle and Bishopston. Pass another waymark post, on the left. Follow the path alongside the Bishopston Pill for a few yards to a waymarked fork in the route. Turn LEFT on a track signposted 'South'. Follow the track up the valley through Lockway Wood. Pass through a gap to the left of a gate and very soon take the left fork (signposted for 'South').

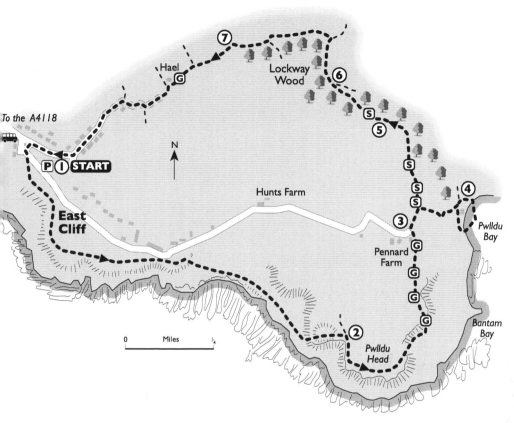

7 At the end of the wood, continue AHEAD on the enclosed track, ignoring a footpath leading off to the right. Pass through a gate and continue AHEAD past the house (Hael). Follow the house access track. Ignore the footpath leading off to the left. At the junction of tracks (by two houses), turn LEFT. Follow the track and then the lane back to the car park/bus stop.

Pwlldu Head

From the car park/bus stop, head seaward for a short distance to the National Trust information sign/waymark posts. Head HALF RIGHT on a well used path and continue roughly parallel to the cliffs, for a range of excellent views, eventually coming in sight of Three Cliffs Bay.

2 Continue to follow the cliffs, to reach a valley with a descent at low tide to the sandy Pobbles Beach. When ready, head inland up the valley for a short way. Look for a wooden boardwalk leading to Pennard Castle. Turn LEFT onto the boardwalk and follow this towards the castle, which soon becomes visible on the skyline. At two waymarked path junctions, follow the signs for the castle. On reaching the castle, the remains of the church can be seen off to the right.

3 When ready, continue along the boardwalk path, soon bearing HALF LEFT to avoid the golf course. Follow a series of small wooden waymark posts until reaching a waymarked junction of paths. Turn LEFT here and descend to the valley alongside Pennard Pill. Turn RIGHT and head along the valley, in due course entering woodland. At a fork in the path, take the right hand (higher) path to reach a waymark sign indicating a right turn for 'Southgate 1m'. (If wishing to visit the café, ignore the right turn and continue AHEAD on the woodland path, which

WEST CLIFFS & PENNARD BURROWS

DESCRIPTION A moderate walk along open access cliff top land, leading to excellent views towards Three Cliffs Bay. This approximately 4¾ mile route then continues along Pennard Burrows (the name 'Burrows' derives from the Norman practice of keeping rabbits in this area) visiting the remains of Pennard Castle. From here, the walk descends to follow Pennard Pill along the valley and through woodland, before returning via the Castle and cliff tops to revisit the views. A short (optional) detour at the midpoint of the route leads to café facilities. Allow about 2¾ hours for the walk.

START Car park at Pennard Cliffs, SS 555874.

PUBLIC TRANSPORT Bus no. 14 from/to Swansea stops adjacent to car park.

Parkmill
A4118
④
Pennard Castle
ruin
③
Walk
N
Pennard Burrows
0 Miles ½
②
Pobbles Beach
Shire Combe
Southgate
START
①

leads round to the right. On reaching a footbridge on the left, cross this and continue AHEAD for a few yards to the road. The café/shop etc. is a short distance away to the left. When ready, follow the outward route back to the 'Southgate 1m' sign and turn LEFT.)

4 Turn RIGHT here and follow the track uphill, bearing RIGHT again on nearing a house. Continue along the path until returning to the edge of the golf course. From this point, continue AHEAD back towards Pennard Castle.

Pass the castle and continue back along the outward route for a further look at the range of views. (At a junction of paths, there is a low tide option of descending to the valley via footpath and using the stepping stones across Pennard Pill to reach the Penmaen Burrows walk on the other side of the valley.)

WALK 8

PARC-LE-BREOS WOODLANDS

DESCRIPTION An easy 3¾ mile walk through deciduous woodlands, owned by Forestry Commission Wales, partly on the Gower Way. An early Neolithic Burial Chamber can be seen alongside the track and a short detour leads to the entrance (locked gate) to Cathole-Rock Cave, where flint tools over 12,000 years old were found. On leaving Parc-le-Breos Woodlands, the route crosses a corner of Cefn Bryn open access land to the village of Penmaen, with a lane and bridleway leading back to the start. Gower Heritage Centre (12th century water mill, museum on the history of Gower and farming in the area, craft workshops and tea-room) lies close to the course of the walk. Allow about 2¼ hours for the walk, plus time to visit the Heritage Centre.

START Forestry Commission Wales parking area, SS 538896.

PUBLIC TRANSPORT Gower Explorer Bus no. 118 from/to Swansea passes along the A4118. Alight at turning for Gower Heritage Centre. Take the lane leading past the shop/café and bear left across a footbridge to the right of a ford. Turn right on lane to reach the start.

1 From the parking area, cross the lane to a small enclosed picnic area, where there is an information board about the Neolithic Burial Chamber. When ready, leave the picnic area, turn LEFT and go through a kissing gate. Follow the track along the valley, towards the burial chamber (to the left of the track). When ready, continue along the track. Pass a structure (possibly a lime kiln) set back in the trees on the right. A short way beyond this, look out for an unmarked path leading uphill on the right. Follow this for a few yards and then take a turning on the right – in a few feet this leads to the entrance to Cathole-Rock Cave.

2 When ready, return to the track and turn RIGHT. Follow the track until reaching a junction of tracks, with a house visible off to the right. Turn LEFT here, following the Gower Way waymark sign (on a short plinth on the right). Follow the stony main track through the woods, ignoring side turnings. On nearing the edge of the woods, at which point the house at Long Oaks can be seen off to the right, turn LEFT on the track which has now become a path.

3 Cross the stile onto Cefn Bryn open access land and turn LEFT on the track. Remain on the main track, which gradually descends towards Penmaen village. At the end of the track, join a lane and follow this through a kissing gate next to a cattlegrid. Continue AHEAD to the junction.

4 Cross the main road with care and take the lane opposite (signed for Three Cliffs Bay Touring Site). Take the left fork at the junction (signed for Caravan Park). Go through the gate at the end of the yellow lines (bridleway sign nearby on left). Go AHEAD between the buildings of North Hills Farm. Follow the lane and then the enclosed track AHEAD. Pass through a gate and continue along the track, which soon descends into woodland and leads to the main road junction near the Gower Heritage Centre. Cross the main road with care and take the lane opposite. Follow this back to the parking area or bus stop.

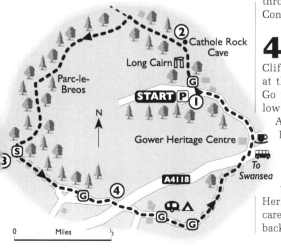

ILSTON CWM & ELIZABETH & ROWE HARDING NATURE RESERVE*

DESCRIPTION A moderate walk of about 5 miles, leading through two areas of woodland, the second of which contains the remains of a pre-reformation chapel which was later used by Baptists as a meeting place. The walk reaches Ilston village via the churchyard. The church dates from the 13thC and a 6thC monastic cell has been found on site. The route continues with a visit to a nearby nature reserve, composed of woodland and the site of a former quarry (the latter an SSSI for the alternating layers of limestone and coal – unique in Wales). A little used lane then leads to the junction with an enclosed bridleway (a good route for butterfly enthusiasts) to Lunnon where a road route is followed back to Parkmill. Allow 3 hours for the walk.

START Gower Heritage Centre, SS 544893 (charge for non-visitors to the Centre)

OR Forestry Commission Wales parking area at Parc-le-Breos, ¼ mile away, SS 538896. If using the latter, return along the lane to the Heritage Centre.

1 From the Heritage Centre, take the road running east through the village, past the shop/café, to the junction with the main road. Cross with care and follow the road to the left for a few yards. Turn RIGHT on a waymarked path that leads over a footbridge. Head up the steps on the left and follow the path through the woodland, climbing two more sets of steps on route.

2 On reaching a waymark sign, head HALF LEFT and then turn RIGHT to follow a path along the lower edge of the wood to the junction with a lane. Turn LEFT and follow the lane to the junction with the main road. Cross the main road with care and head RIGHT, passing an outdoor activity centre.

3 Just before reaching the public house, turn LEFT on a waymarked bridleway that runs just to the left of the pub car park. On reaching the end of the car park, bear HALF RIGHT on a path that leads across an open area and back into trees. Cross a footbridge and follow the main path AHEAD.

4 Cross a second footbridge, just after which the remains of the chapel can be seen on the right. When ready, continue along the bridleway, soon taking the right fork. Bear RIGHT on reaching a waymark post (the other path is overgrown at time of writing). Cross a further footbridge and follow the path to the right. Take a further right fork to reach the next footbridge.

5 Keep to the main (well-used) path through the wood, crossing a fifth footbridge and following the path to the left. Turn LEFT at the waymark sign and cross another footbridge. Follow the path to a kissing gate into the churchyard. When ready, exit the churchyard by the main gate to the village, crossing a footbridge to reach the road. Turn RIGHT on the road. At the junction, continue AHEAD. Ignore, for the moment, a narrow lane leading up to the left. Continue along the road, past several houses.

6 Look for a ford on the left, leading to a stile into the nature reserve. Within the reserve are a number of 'there-and-back-again' paths, including one to the site of the former quarry and one that leads uphill to a pool. When ready, return across the ford and head RIGHT back towards the village. On reaching the narrow lane passed earlier, turn RIGHT and follow this apparently little used route to the junction by the entrance to Bryn-afel.

7 Follow the road to the left. On reaching the turning for Furzehill (on the right), turn LEFT onto an enclosed bridleway. Follow the track between hedges to join the road at the edge of Lunnon village. Turn RIGHT and follow the road past a side-turning on the left to reach a junction. Turn LEFT and follow the road down to Parkmill.

✱ This walk can be combined with 'Gelli-hir

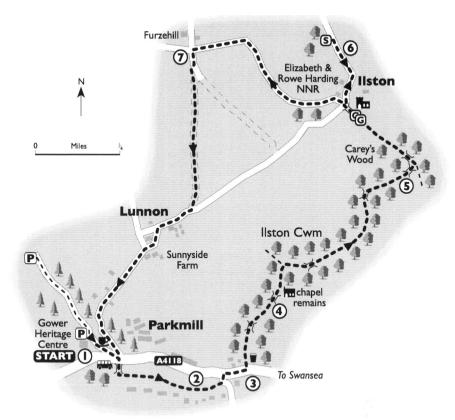

Wood' by following the attractive lane north from Ilston and turning RIGHT at the junction with the B4271. The alternative footpath route across the common towards the 'Gellihir' turning, although waymarked, can be difficult going after wet weather.

Gower Heritage
Centre

WALK 10
CEFN BRYN & ARTHUR'S STONE

DESCRIPTION A moderate hill walk of some 6¼ miles along a ridge near the middle of Gower. The route passes a viewpoint, a prehistoric burial chamber (Arthur's Stone, with a capstone weighing over 25 tons) and has an optional extension of about 1½ miles there and back, to visit a local public house at Reynoldston. With a range of great views, covering much of the Gower peninsula, this walk is perhaps best left to last – many of the other routes in this guide can be seen from a distance while following this walk. Allow about 3¾ hours.

START Picnic area/small car park at SS 528887.

PUBLIC TRANSPORT Gower Explorer bus no.118 stops near Penmaen church. Follow the lane to the right of the church for about ¼ mile. After crossing the cattle grid, look for the waymarked bridleway track leading half right and join the walk at this point. This walk can be shortened by catching a 118 bus from outside the pub at Reynoldston, either back to Penmaen or to Swansea (see Gower Explorer timetables for full details).

1 Face away from the picnic area/car park and head RIGHT along the lane. On reaching a waymarked bridleway track on the left, turn on to this. At a junction of tracks, with a Gower Way Plinth to the right, take the left fork. Ascend the rise, as sea views come in sight on the left.

2 At a fork in the track, near a boulder on the left, take the left fork. The boulder holds an inscription plate for Gower Way. Follow the track around the curve of the hill, now with a view of Oxwich Bay on the left, to rejoin the other track and turn LEFT on this. Pass to the left of a building and fenced-in area and cross slightly lower ground to reach a junction of tracks, with a Gower Way Plinth on the left.

3 Continue AHEAD on a track that ascends the next rise, while tending gradually to the left. Cross the next rise, at which point Rhossili Down and the adjacent hills come into view. At the next junction, continue AHEAD, passing a Gower Way Plinth on the right. Continue along the main track, looking out for the Rotary Club Celebration Plinths on the right. The circular plinth gives directions and distances to a range of places in Britain.

4 Return to the main track and continue along this to the unfenced road. Cross the road (a left turn on the road at this point will lead to the public house at Reynoldston) and leave the Gower Way at this point, following a track leading directly ahead towards Arthur's Stone (the capstone is visible at this point). Follow the track past pools to reach the burial chamber. To return to the road, follow a grassy track curving round to the right – Broad Pool, a nature reserve, can be seen on the lower ground off to the left.

5 On rejoining the road (a right turn on the road at this point will lead to the public house at Reynoldston), cross this and follow the waymarked track AHEAD. Continue AHEAD over junctions of track for about 1½ miles to the junction with the Gower Way (Gower Way Plinth on right. This is the junction at the start of stage **3** above). Follow the Gower Way and subsequent tracks back to the car park/bus stop.

⬛ Arthur's Stone

⑤ ④

N

0   Miles   ½

To Swansea

③ ② **Penmaen** START 🅿①

A4118

14

WALK 11

PENMAEN BURROWS

DESCRIPTION A moderate 3½ mile walk, with two main ascents, via woodlands, lane and paths to Penmaen Burrows. A circuit of this open access cliff top land passes near an earthwork, a pillow mound (used for rabbit farming in Norman times), a burial chamber and the remains of a chapel, as well as great views east and west. Two beaches can be reached at low tide, within a short distance of this walk. There are also linking paths to two other coastal walks in this guide. Allow about 2 hours for the walk.

START Gower Heritage Centre, SS 544893 (charge for non-visitors to the Centre) OR Forestry Commission Wales parking area at Parc-le-Breos, ¼ mile away, SS 538896. If using the latter, return along lane to the Heritage Centre.

PUBLIC TRANSPORT Gower Explorer Bus no. 118 from/to Swansea passes along the A4118, near the Gower Heritage Centre.

1 From the Heritage Centre, follow the lane to the main road. Head RIGHT with care for a short distance, to join a waymarked bridleway on the left of the road. Follow this uphill through woodlands (carpeted with wild garlic in spring). At the end of the wood, continue AHEAD on the enclosed track. Pass through a gate across the track and continue AHEAD. Pass North Hills Farm, going through the left hand gate, and follow the lane AHEAD to a T-junction. Turn LEFT at the junction.

2 After a short while, come to Notthill (National Trust land) on the left. Bear LEFT on a path through this small area of woodland. At the end of the woodland, continue AHEAD. Ignore the first path leading off to the right (for the moment) and continue to the second junction of paths. Turn RIGHT and follow the path to

a bench and viewpoint. When ready, return to the junction of paths, turn LEFT and then LEFT again at the next junction. Follow the path past a bench and down steps to the lane. Turn LEFT on the lane and follow this for a short way to a waymarked path leading right. Follow the path downhill, across a footbridge and up to the top of Penmaen Burrows.

3 Turn LEFT on a path running around the summit of Penmaen Burrows, passing features such as earthwork, pillow mound, remains of burial chamber and church, as well as a range of excellent views. On completing the circuit, descend on outward route, cross footbridge and follow path up to lane. Turn LEFT and follow the lane to the turning for North Hill Farm. Follow bridleway past the farm and back to the junction near Gower Heritage Centre.

Note
• A footpath route, with stepping stones that can be accessed at low tide, leads east from this walk to that along Pennard Burrows.
• Three Cliffs and Nicholaston Beaches can be easily reached from this walk at low tide.
• The footpath shown as running alongside Pennard Pill

and through Northill Wood (an alternative route back to Gower Heritage Centre) can be very muddy and slippery in its riverside sections and is only really suitable for dry weather walking.

NICHOLASTON BURROWS, BEACH & WOODS

DESCRIPTION Starting from near Penmaen, this moderate 3¾ mile walk follows a lane and track to join the Gower Coast Path on Penmaen Burrows, with views of the sea. Descending through deciduous woodland, the route then heads across the dunes to the beach and follows this to a footbridge link with the 'Oxwich Burrows and Beach' walk opposite. Turning back towards the east, the walk now winds its way through the burrows, at the foot of attractive escarpments. An alternative footpath route is followed back to the road near Penmaen. Allow about 2¼ hours for the walk.

START Picnic area/small car park at SS 528887 OR the bus stop at SS 527885.

PUBLIC TRANSPORT Gower Explorer no. 118 bus service from/to Swansea passes along the A4118 at Penmaen (using the bus service shortens the walk by about ½ mile).

1 From the parking area, follow the lane west (away from Penmaen Church) to reach the junction with the main road. Cross the road with care and head RIGHT for a short distance to a waymarked gate on the left (if arriving by bus, join the walk at this point) Go through the gate and go straight AHEAD on the track that eventually becomes a concrete path. Go through another gate and take the right fork in the path.

2 Follow the path as this veers round to the right above the cliffs. Pass an old limekiln and go through a gate. Follow the path round to the right. On reaching a three-way waymark post, continue AHEAD (signed for Coast Path and Nicholaston Woods). Ignore the stile on the right and continue along the path. Just after passing a second stile on the right (now marked as 'Private'), turn LEFT on a path that runs down through the woods to emerge at Nicholaston Burrows.

3 Head across the dunes on one of the paths leading to the beach. Turn RIGHT and follow the beach until nearing the point where a stream runs out into the sea. Turn RIGHT and follow the stream until nearing a footbridge. DO NOT CROSS THE FOOTBRIDGE BUT TURN RIGHT on a path which gradually curves to the left to reach a waymark post. Continue along the path, which generally tends half left, passing a number of waymark posts and with rock outcroppings off to the left.

4 Follow the waymarked route back into woodland and continue to follow a series of waymark signs until reaching an Oxwich National Nature Reserve information board on the left. Turn SHARP RIGHT at this point and follow a path that leads out of the woods to the dunes. Turn LEFT and head along the dunes. Towards the end of the dunes, turn LEFT and head back up through the woods to the path from Penmaen Burrows (there are a number of paths up through the wood – follow any of these and turn RIGHT on the path at the top of the wood).

5 Return along the path as far as the three-way waymark post passed in stage **2** above. Go through the gate, following the sign for Penmaen. Follow a path through bracken for some way, and then go through an open gateway on the right. Turn LEFT and follow the path through a gate and along a field, with fencing off to the left. Go through a gate and turn LEFT to go through a second gate onto the A4188. The bus stop is roughly opposite and the lane to the car park is a short distance away to the right.

To Swanse

A4118

Penmaen

N

Nicholaston Burrows

Link to Oxwich Burrows

0   Miles   ¼

16

WALK 13

OXWICH BURROWS & BEACH

DESCRIPTION An easy 3 mile walk on a waymarked route through the dunes at Oxwich Burrows (part of the National Nature Reserve) with views towards Oxwich Marsh (there is restricted access to that part of the reserve). On nearing the footbridge link to the 'Nicholaston Burrows, Beach and Woods' walk opposite the route then bears right to Oxwich Beach and follows this back to the start. Allow about 1¾ hours for the walk.

START Parking area (charge) adjacent to Oxwich Beach, SS 501865.

PUBLIC TRANSPORT Gower Explorer Bus Service no. 118 from/to Swansea stops on the road adjacent to car park and café.

2 Turn RIGHT on the sandy track. Pass through a gate and continue AHEAD on the track, going HALF LEFT at a waymark post. Follow the now grassy track, going AHEAD at a further waymark post. Take the right fork at a third waymark post. Pass through a kissing gate and follow the grassy track AHEAD. At a fork in the track, bear SLIGHTLY TO THE RIGHT (away from the trees) and soon head towards the next waymark post.

3 Pass through a small area of trees and continue AHEAD to the next waymark post. Bear LEFT and then RIGHT at the next fork. Go through a kissing gate and follow the path HALF LEFT. Bear towards the LEFT at the next two waymark posts. Before reaching a ridge of slightly higher ground, bear RIGHT on a sandy track that soon leads to a footbridge (the link to the 'Nicholaston Burrows, Beach and Woods' walk).

1 Near the entrance to the car park, join a path running north roughly parallel to the road into Oxwich (the light coloured path is surfaced with crushed shells). Take the left fork, continuing to follow the 'shell' route. Ignore a stile on the left and continue to follow the path to a kissing gate. Continue along the path until reaching a junction with a sandy track, at which point the shells cease.

4 DO NOT CROSS THE FOOTBRIDGE. Turn RIGHT and follow the stream towards Oxwich Beach, with views towards the cliffs on the left. Turn RIGHT and follow the beach back towards the car park/bus stop.

WALK 14

OXWICH HEADLAND

DESCRIPTION An energetic 4¾ mile walk (with two main ascents) following a path past St Illtyd's Church and through coastal woodland, before emerging to continue along open ground past some impressive limestone outcrops. On reaching the small beach at The Sands, the route then turns inland, following a track and then quiet lanes back towards Oxwich. On nearing the village, a short section of footpath leads close to Oxwich Castle (owned by Cadw and with an admission charge). The final lane descent passes the ivy-covered remains of an old dovecote. Allow about 2¾ hours for the walk, plus time to visit castle if required.

START Parking area (subject to charge) adjacent to Oxwich Beach, SS 501865.

PUBLIC TRANSPORT Gower Explorer Bus Service no. 118 from/to Swansea stops on the road adjacent to the car park and café.

I From the car park/bus stop head for a few yards into Oxwich, to reach the crossroads. Turn LEFT and follow the no-through lane to the end. Continue AHEAD on the tarmac and then the unsurfaced path to reach the entrance to St Illtyd's Church. After visiting the church continue along the path that runs to the left of the churchyard. Pass a National Nature Reserve Information Board on the right and bear RIGHT up a long flight of steps (there is a bench about half way up).

2 On reaching a waymarked junction of paths, turn LEFT on the Coast Path/path to Oxwich Point. Follow the main path through the woods and then between woods and a field (there is a trig point in field off to the right). Continue along the path, which soon descends back towards the sea's edge. Continue to follow the path to eventually

exit the wood. Continue AHEAD to reach a kissing gate with another National Nature Reserve Information Board nearby.

3 Beyond the kissing gate, follow the path AHEAD. Take the left fork at a waymark post, following the sign for Coast Path/Horton. Follow the path round Oxwich Point, with Port-Eynon Bay now coming into view. At the next waymark post, continue to follow the route for the Coast Path/Horton. Pass a stile, a gate and a second stile and follow the path to the left of the fence. Pass a disused stile, soon after which the small bay, The Sands, is reached.

4 From here, cross a stile and follow the path leading inland (this route currently forms part of a footpath diversion). Cross another stile and turn LEFT. Follow the track AHEAD and then round to the right. Pass through a kissing gate and bear RIGHT on a track and then lane leading up The Slade. At the T-junction, turn RIGHT and follow the quiet lane (with sea views to the right). Ignore the bridleway sign on the left and continue to follow the lane to and through Oxwich Green. Continue to follow the lane (now with a view towards Cefn Bryn) until reaching a junction.

5 Cross the stone stile on the right and head across the field towards Oxwich Castle. Cross a second stile and turn LEFT on the track. The entrance to the castle is on the right, beyond the car park. When ready, return to the track and head RIGHT down to the lane. Turn RIGHT and follow the lane downhill, ignoring footpath signs on the right. Look out for the old dovecote, also on the right. At the crossroads, continue AHEAD back towards the car park/bus stop.

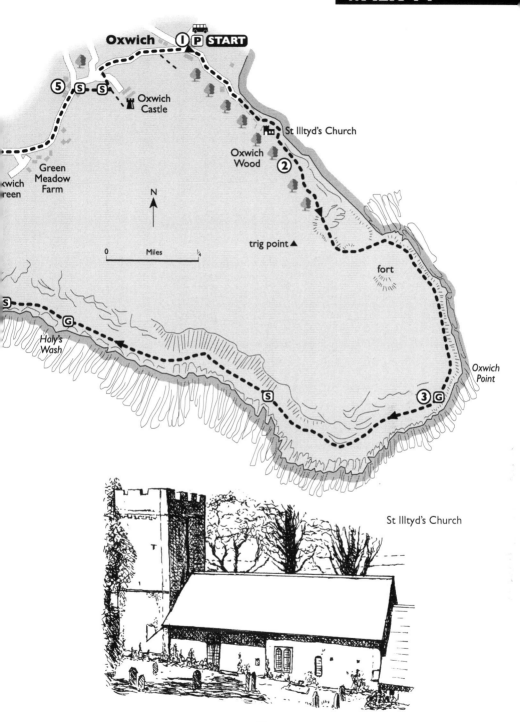

Oxwich

① P START

⑤ Ⓢ Ⓢ

Oxwich Castle

Green Meadow Farm

xwich reen

St Illtyd's Church

Oxwich Wood

②

N

0 — Miles — ¼

trig point ▲

fort

Ⓢ

Ⓖ

Holy's Wash

Oxwich Point

Ⓢ

③ Ⓖ

St Illtyd's Church

PORT-EYNON BAY

DESCRIPTION This moderate 3½ mile walk begins by going along the beach at Port Eynon Bay, with views of the attractive headlands on either side. A complete contrast follows, as the route turns inland to follow a footpath up a treelined valley, before following a track with hill views to Eastern Slade. Descending another valley, the walk joins the Gower Coast Path to return to Port-Eynon Bay and retrace the outward route along the beach. Allow about 2 hours for the walk.
START Car park at Port Eynon, SS 467852.
PUBLIC TRANSPORT Gower Explorer bus no. 118, from/to Swansea, stops in Port Eynon, near the car park.

1 From the car park/bus stop, head past the roundabout to the beach. Turn LEFT and follow the beach, with views inland towards the dunes and hills beyond, as well as the coastline ahead. On nearing the end of the beach, look out for a flight of wooden steps on the left. Cross the dunes by means of the steps and cross the small green beyond to a lane.

2 Turn RIGHT and follow the lane to the end. At this point, turn LEFT and go through a small gate (currently painted green) just to the right of a garage. Follow the path up through woodland and continue AHEAD until reaching a junction of rights of way, with a stone stile to the left.

3 Do not cross the stile. Turn RIGHT and follow a track that leads, via a kissing gate, to the farm at Western Slade. Pass between the house and the other buildings. Continue to follow the track, passing through a gate (which may be open) to reach a lane junction at Eastern Slade.

4 Turn RIGHT and descend the lane, going through an opening to the right of the road gate. Continue down the track. At a fork in the right of way, take the right hand route, soon going through a gate. Follow the track until reaching a stile on the left. Cross this and follow the path AHEAD to a second stile.

5 Turn RIGHT and follow the Coast Path, crossing a walkway and a stone stile, to reach a gate onto the lane from stage **2** of this walk. Follow the lane back to the small green, cross this and follow the path back to the beach. Turn RIGHT and follow the beach back to Port Eynon.

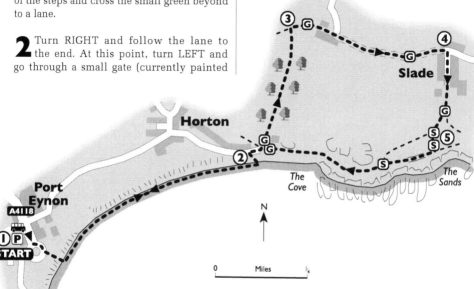

WALK 16

PORT EYNON HEADLAND & OVERTON CLIFF

DESCRIPTION A beach walk from Port Eynon passes the local Youth Hostel and the remains of the Salt House before ascending the headland to the monument to Gwent Jones and Stephen Lee. A meandering path leads along the headland, with a short detour to look down on Culver Hole (a man made cave, stronghold for Port Eynon castle and later used by smugglers), before following the coast path through cliff land owned by Glamorgan Wildlife Trust – there are some spectacular outcroppings on this section. The last stage of the walk follows the coast path inland and then returns to Port Eynon via bridleway, lane and footpath. This moderate walk is 3 miles in length, for which about 1¾ hours should be allowed.

START Car park at Port Eynon, SS 467852.
PUBLIC TRANSPORT Gower Explorer bus no. 118, from/to Swansea, stops in Port Eynon, near the car park.

1 From the car park/bus stop, head past the roundabout to the beach. Turn RIGHT and follow the beach past the first house towards the Youth Hostel. Immediately before reaching the Youth Hostel, turn RIGHT on a waymarked path (signed for Port Eynon Point ⅓ m). In a few yards, take the left fork in the path. After another few yards, turn LEFT onto a permissive path that leads across a field with touring caravan pitches.

2 Go through a gate at the far side to pass the remains of the Salt House on the left. Beyond this, bear RIGHT and follow a stony path up to the top of the headland, passing small quarry areas on route, to reach the hilltop monument, from where there are excellent views. When ready, follow a grassy track leading away from the monument, along the left hand side

of the ridge. Bear LEFT for a view down to Culver Hole.

3 Retrace the outward route for a few yards, then bear LEFT on a path that winds between patches of gorse. Ignore paths leading downhill to the left until reaching a point where the main track makes a sharp right turn. Turn LEFT onto a descending path at this point and soon turn LEFT again. At the bottom of the hill, go through a gate.

4 Head RIGHT along the path across the valley. Descend a flight of steps on the left and follow the path to a gate, adjacent to which is a Glamorgan Wildlife Trust sign. Follow the path along below Overton Cliffs to reach a further gate. Pass through this and turn RIGHT. Follow the path uphill and between large outcroppings to reach a Coast Path waymark post at a junction of tracks. Turn RIGHT and follow the bridleway through a gate and along an enclosed track. At the end of the track, go through a gate and follow a lane to the left. At a road junction, take the right fork.

5 Just after passing New House Farm (on the right), turn RIGHT over a way-marked stile. Cross the field to a second stile. Continue AHEAD, aiming just to the left of a telegraph pole, to reach a third stile. Cross and join a tarmac route, bearing LEFT on this. Follow the access route through the caravan site to reach the road. Turn RIGHT to very soon reach the car park/bus stop.

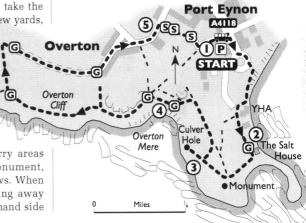

21

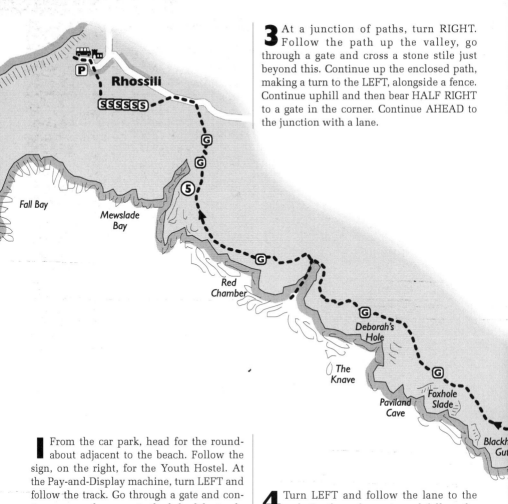

3 At a junction of paths, turn RIGHT. Follow the path up the valley, go through a gate and cross a stone stile just beyond this. Continue up the enclosed path, making a turn to the LEFT, alongside a fence. Continue uphill and then bear HALF RIGHT to a gate in the corner. Continue AHEAD to the junction with a lane.

I From the car park, head for the round-about adjacent to the beach. Follow the sign, on the right, for the Youth Hostel. At the Pay-and-Display machine, turn LEFT and follow the track. Go through a gate and continue across the grass, to the left of the track. Head for the far left corner of the camping field, beyond which the Youth Hostel building can be seen. Descend stone steps to the footpath alongside the Youth Hostel.

2 Turn RIGHT and follow the path, going AHEAD at a junction of paths. At junctions of paths, follow signs for Overton. Follow the track up onto more open ground on Port Eynon headland, passing some interesting rock outcrops on the right. When the track bends to the left, descend a side path leading HALF RIGHT. Follow the path through a gate and continue AHEAD for a few yards.

4 Turn LEFT and follow the lane to the end. Go through a gate and follow the enclosed bridleway track along the hill. Go through a gate and continue AHEAD to a three-way waymark post, at which point the Gower Coast Path is joined. This section of the route generally keeps fairly close to the boundary of the farmland on the right, although diversions to the left are possible on the open access sections of the route. In the latter stages of the walk there are also paths leading down to some of the beaches, while the coast path crosses the valleys leading down to the coastline. There are seven gates on this section of the walk and wooden marker posts indicate the route on open hill land.

5 In about 3 miles, descend to the valley leading to Mewslade Bay (worth a visit at low tide if time allows), pass through a gate, leave the coast path and head RIGHT on a path that soon leads through another gate and up a track to the road at Middleton. Turn LEFT and follow the road, soon joining a pavement on the left. Shortly after passing the entrance to a lane on the right, turn LEFT on an enclosed track. At a fork in the route, bear RIGHT. Cross six stiles.

6 On reaching a seventh stile, do not cross this but continue AHEAD. On reaching the junction with the road, turn LEFT and follow the road towards Rhossili. The bus shelter will be seen on the right, with the cafés, shops and Visitor Centre further along the road.

WALK 17
PORT EYNON TO RHOSSILI

DESCRIPTION This energetic 5¾ mile linear coastal walk leads via footpath, lane and bridleway to join the Gower Coast Path to the west of Overton. With a range of great sea views, the fairly level grassy track leads through nature reserves and across open access land. After the mid-point of the walk, near Foxhole Slade, there are descents and ascents on the coast path, which allow access to some attractive bays at low tide. The final section of the walk turns inland to follow footpaths via Middleton to Rhossili, where there are cafes, shops and a National Trust Visitor Centre. Allow about 3¾ hours for the walk, plus time to visit the beaches if you wish.
START Car park at Port Eynon, SS 467852.
PUBLIC TRANSPORT Gower Explorer bus no. 118, from/to Swansea, operates between Rhossili and Port Eynon. This service is also suitable for those who wish to reverse the direction of the walk.

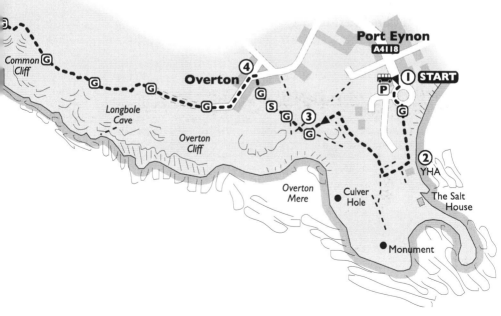

WALK 18

MEWSLADE BAY, FALL BAY & WORM'S HEAD

DESCRIPTION From Rhossili village, where there is a National Trust Visitor Centre and a variety of cafés and shops, this moderate 4½ mile walk follows a mainly off-road route to the neighbouring village of Middleton. This section of the walk passes through fields in which traces of the medieval 'strip' system of farming can be seen. From Middleton, the route joins the Gower Coast Path, from which Mewslade and Fall Bays can be accessed at low tide. On reaching the headland near the Lookout Station, where there is an excellent view of Worm's Head, the walk joins the Gower Way for an easy walk back to Rhossili village. Allow about 2½ hours for the walk.

START Car park at SS 414881 or bus stop at SS 415882.

PUBLIC TRANSPORT Gower Explorer bus no. 118, from/to Swansea, stops near the church.

1 From the car park head inland for a short distance towards the church (if arriving by bus, join the walk at the point where it passes the bus stop). Pass the bus stop and take the right fork in the road. Take the second turn on the right, by a waymark sign on telegraph pole and a red litter bin. In a few yards, reach a junction of tracks and take the right fork. Follow the enclosed track until reaching a Tir Gofal waymark sign on a stile on the left.

2 Cross the stile and follow the left hand side of the field to a stile onto a

track. Turn LEFT and follow the waymarked footpath route, mostly between hedges and crossing another two stiles. After the second stile, take the right hand fork in the footpath. Cross a further six stiles on the waymarked route. On reaching a junction, turn LEFT and follow the track to the junction with the road at Middleton.

3 Turn RIGHT and follow the pavement through the village. At the end of the pavement, continue along the right hand side of the road for a few yards. Turn RIGHT on a path signed for 'Mewslade ½'. Follow the enclosed path, looking for a notice on a gate to the right, about the management of the field for wildlife encouragement purposes. Continue along the track and go through a gate onto National Trust land.

4 Bear RIGHT on the Gower Coast Path and follow this for about 1¾ miles to the junction with the Gower Way near the Lookout Station. On this section of the route, optional detours can be made to the adjacent headlands and, at low tide, to visit Mewslade and Fall Bays, afterwards returning to the main route.

5 From near the Lookout Station, join the track leading between cliff and enclosed fields to return to Rhossili village. Pass through a gate and join the road near the National Trust Visitor Centre and car park. The bus stop is a short way further up the road.

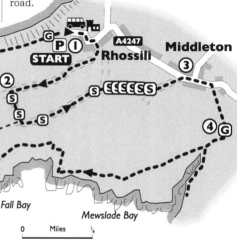

24

WALK 19
RHOSSILI DOWN & BEACH

DESCRIPTION From Rhossili village, this 4½ mile walk passes near the village church (where there is a Memorial to Petty Officer Evans, a member of Scott's 1912 Antarctic Expedition) and climbs up to The Beacon on Rhossili Down. The bridleway route along the Down allows a range of excellent views over the sea and adjacent land, before descending towards Hillend Burrows. Another bridleway, along the base of Rhossili Down can be used for the return journey, but – for better views towards the Down – a walk through Hillend Burrows leads to Rhossili Beach, which can be followed back to Rhossili village. Allow about 2¾ hours for the walk.

START Car park at SS 414881 or bus stop at SS 415882.

PUBLIC TRANSPORT Gower Explorer bus no. 118, from/to Swansea, stops near the church.

I From the car park/bus stop, head inland for a short distance towards the church. After visiting the church, if wished, follow the path running to the left of the churchyard. Turn LEFT on meeting the junction with a track, passing a standing stone on the small green to the right. Ignore the waymarked gate on the left and continue AHEAD to a second way-marked gate, leading onto Rhossili Down. Go through the second gate and head uphill, to the right of a small building. Go up steps and continue to climb to reach the Beacon trig point.

2 Continue along the ridge for about 1¼ miles, keeping to the main track, and then descend, bearing gradually towards the left to reach a gate to a lane near Hillend Burrows Caravan and Camping site. (If you wish to follow the bridleway along the base of Rhossili Down, do not go through the gate but turn SHARP LEFT and follow the way-marked bridleway track. Rejoin the outward route near the church).

3 To continue on the main route, go through the gate and turn LEFT. Follow the signed route to the car park area at Hillend Burrows. Follow a fenced walkway to the right of the parking area and continue AHEAD through the dunes to the beach. Turn LEFT and follow the beach back towards Rhossili. The Old Rectory (at the base of the Down), Worm's Head and adjacent cliffs are among the views on route.

4 On nearing the cliffs at the far end of the beach, turn LEFT and go up steps. Bear RIGHT through a gate and follow the path to another gate. Pass through and continue AHEAD to the junction with the road. Turn LEFT for the bus stop and RIGHT for the car park.

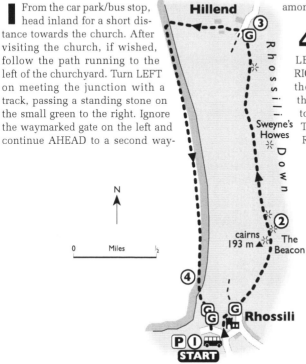

25

RHOSSILI TO REYNOLDSTON

DESCRIPTION This moderate 5¼ mile linear walk starts with an ascent part way up Rhossili Down, before following the Gower Way along the eastern side of the ridge, with views towards the hills further north. Still following the Gower Way, the route then heads east through lowland fields and along old farm tracks to reach St David's Church and the small village of Llanddewi. A main road section leads to the neighbouring village of Knelston, where the route leaves the Gower Way to follow a little used lane. Once beyond the few houses, the lane is edged with attractive trees and hedgerows. Crossing a stile onto Frog Moor, on the edge of Cefn Bryn, the route then leads up across the common land, to join an unfenced road leading east to Reynoldston. The walk ends near the King Arthur Hotel. Allow about 3 hours for the walk, plus time to visit the church and public house if you wish.
START Car park at SS 414881 or bus stop at SS 415882.
PUBLIC TRANSPORT Gower Explorer 118, running between Reynoldston and Rhossili, stops at the roadside near the King Arthur.

1 From the car park/bus stop, head inland for a short distance towards the church. After visiting the church, if wished, follow the path running to the left of the churchyard. Turn LEFT on meeting the junction with a track, passing a standing stone on the small green to the right. Ignore the waymarked gate on the left and continue AHEAD to a second waymarked gate, leading onto Rhossili Down. Go through the second gate and head uphill, to the right of a small building. Continue to follow the route uphill, going up a set of steps, with a Gower Way waymark sign on the top step. Continue to ascend, until Burry Holms headland comes into view, ahead and to the left.

2 At this point, bear HALF RIGHT, keeping to the left of the bracken. Soon bear HALF RIGHT again, towards a fence and old drystone wall. Bear LEFT along the open ground, keeping quite close to the fence and wall, with views right towards the coast. Pass a house, off to the right, and continue AHEAD until reaching a fenced off building (connected with the reservoir on the map). Pass to the left of this and continue AHEAD. Descend gradually to the RIGHT to join the stony track near Fernhill Farm. Turn LEFT and follow the track for some way along the edge of Rhossili Down, with views towards the hills ahead.

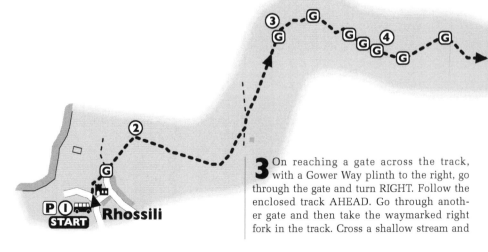

3 On reaching a gate across the track, with a Gower Way plinth to the right, go through the gate and turn RIGHT. Follow the enclosed track AHEAD. Go through another gate and then take the waymarked right fork in the track. Cross a shallow stream and then follow the track to the left of the old farm buildings at Kingshall. Go through a waymarked gate and follow the grassy track along the right hand side of the field. Pass through a further gate and continue AHEAD for a few yards, then bear LEFT, following the bridleway signs that lead along the left hand boundary of the field to a waymarked gate in the corner.

4 Follow the enclosed track to another gate, pass through and follow a grassy track diagonally across the field to a gate on the far side. Head along the next section of enclosed track, which soon leads to the right of the farm buildings at Old Henllys. Go through a gate and follow the track to the left of the house. Ignore the footpath leading off to the left and continue along the track, which bears left near a pond on the right. On reaching a junction of tracks (near New Henllys), continue STRAIGHT AHEAD, going through a gate into an enclosed track.

5 Continue STRAIGHT AHEAD along the track (an old quarry is visible off to the right), with Cefn Bryn coming into view ahead. Pass a house, off to the right. Follow the track past farm buildings, looking out for the gate into St David's churchyard on the left. After visiting the church, if wished, return to the farm track and continue along this. When the track bends sharply to the left,

6 Follow the main road, with care (it is a narrow verge and traffic can be fast) through the village of Knelston. Continue past the school (on the left) to reach a no-through lane on the left, opposite a garage/shop. Turn LEFT into the lane and follow this to the very end, where a stile leads onto the open access land at Frog Moor. Follow tracks and paths leading HALF RIGHT up the common, towards a white house on the right. Pass the house and continue up the common, to join the unfenced road just to the left of other houses. Turn RIGHT and follow the road to Reynoldston. After passing the Post Office/shop (on the right) look for a track leading across open ground on the right, towards the King Arthur Hotel. The bus back to Rhossili can be caught from the roadside near the turning for the King Arthur.

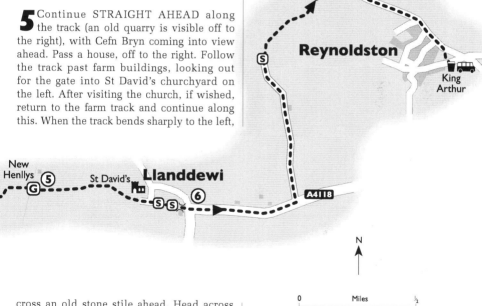

cross an old stone stile ahead. Head across the field, aiming just to the left of a house on the far side. After crossing a small ridge in the field, head towards a stile and footbridge leading to a road. Turn RIGHT and almost immediately turn LEFT on the main road.

LLANGENNITH BURROWS & MOORS

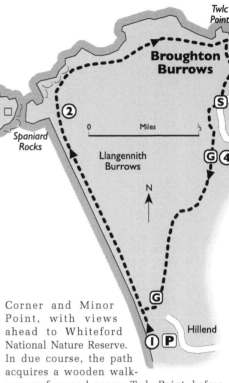

DESCRIPTION A varied and easy walk of some 3¼ miles, following a beach route that passes near Burry Holms, site of an Iron Age earthwork and a medieval chapel. From here, the route joins the Gower Coast Path, passing around the headland to a view over Broughton Bay and Whiteford National Nature Reserve. Turning inland, the route skirts Llangennith Moors, beyond which Rhossili Down and Llanmadoc Hill can be seen, before returning via dunes to the parking area. Allow about 2 hours for the walk. Llangennith village, about one mile away, is also worth visiting, as the site of the largest church in Gower (St Cennydd's). On a nearby green are the remains of St Cennydd's Well. The village pub is a short distance away.

START Hillend car park (charge) about one mile from Llangennith village in a south-westerly direction, SS 413909.

PUBLIC TRANSPORT Gower Explorer Bus Service no. 115 from and to Llanrhidian (with a connection to Swansea) stops at Llangennith village. Alight at the turning for Hillend Burrows and follow the lane to the left (this is the bus stop after the one by the church and pub). Arriving by bus adds about 2 miles to the walk's length.

1 From the Hillend car park, join the waymarked footpath situated towards the right hand side of the car park. Follow the walkway between fences and continue AHEAD to the beach. Turn RIGHT and follow the beach towards Burry Holms and Spaniard Rocks.

2 On reaching the rocky line of Spaniard Rocks, bear RIGHT and join the waymarked Gower Coast Path as this heads up into the dunes (the flotsam at the tide line can be noticeable, but is soon left behind). Follow the waymarked route along through the dunes, passing Three Chimneys, Bluepool Corner and Minor Point, with views ahead to Whiteford National Nature Reserve. In due course, the path acquires a wooden walkway surface and passes Twlc Point, before turning right towards the caravan site at Broughton Farm.

3 Follow the path down towards the caravan site, heading RIGHT at the three-way waymark post. Bear RIGHT at the next junction, following the waymarked driveway to a small car park on the right. Continue along the lane past the car park and cross a stile on the right, just to the right of a gate. Follow the track AHEAD, then through bends to left and right.

4 Pass through a kissing gate and continue along the track, now with views to Llangennith Moors on the left and Llanmadoc Hill beyond. On reaching a two-way waymark post, continue AHEAD. Go through a gate and bear RIGHT on a path running to the right of a stream. On reaching the beach, turn LEFT. Follow the beach back to the path through the dunes to the car park and thence back to Llangennith village.

WALK 22

BROUGHTON BAY

DESCRIPTION A generally easy walk of about 4 miles that can best be enjoyed at low tide. A lane, and then track, route leads from the village of Llanmadoc, past the enclosed Lagadranta sand dunes, to Broughton Bay with its wide sandy beach, backed by rocky tors. A walk along the beach, bearing west towards the ridge of higher ground, and then back to the east, passing Prissen's and Hill's Tors, brings Cwm Ivy Tor (beyond dunes) into view. A path leads through the dunes to join the track and then lane back up to Llanmadoc village, skirting the edge of Whiteford National Nature Reserve on route. Allow some 2½ hours for the walk.

START Car park at SS 440935 or car park at SS 427933* (see instruction 2).

PUBLIC TRANSPORT Gower Explorer Bus Services 115 and 116 (usually with a change of buses at Cilibion or Llanrhidian Cross). Bus stop is at the village green.

1 From the Cwm Ivy car park, follow the lane back up hill to the junction by the church and turn RIGHT (from the bus stop, continue west along the lane, passing a second green on the left, to reach the junction by the church and take the left fork). The no-through lane is signposted for Broughton Beach parking. Follow the lane for about ¾ mile, ignoring a permissive route leading off to the right.

2 Cross a cattlegrid, soon after which, turn RIGHT on a track that leads past a shop and a car park* and then continues through open ground. Follow the track through a turn to the left and go through two waymarked kissing gates. Beyond the second gate, continue AHEAD on a path through a short stretch of dunes to the beach.

3 Start by bearing LEFT to take in the views of the higher ground at the end of the beach. When ready, turn back and follow the beach past the outcroppings of Prissen's and Hill's Tors. On reaching the start of the dunes, on the right, look for a small sign at the edge of these. Follow the path through the dunes (please keep to the path, as there are ground nesting birds in this area).

4 After about ¼ mile, turn RIGHT on a track that leads to a kissing gate near Cwm Ivy Tor. Go through the gate and turn LEFT on the track. Follow the track uphill, passing through a gate out of National Trust land. Just beyond this, turn LEFT and then follow the lane back uphill to the Cwm Ivy car park and Llanmadoc village.

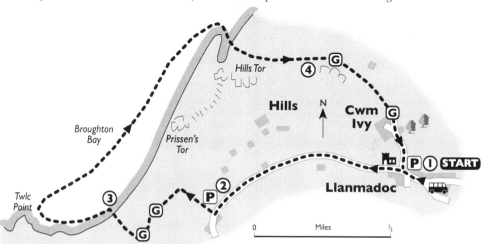

WHITEFORD NATIONAL NATURE RESERVE

DESCRIPTION An easy 4 mile walk, taking about 2½ hours. Starting from the village of Llanmadoc, the walk leads by lane and then track to Whiteford Sands. After heading north along the beach for about 1 mile, the route passes near an old iron lighthouse and the Burry inlet, with the south Carmarthenshire coast beyond. Swinging round to the right, the walk then follows a winding route along Whiteford Burrows, then passes between forestry and Cwm Ivy freshwater marsh. The outward track and lane route is used to return to the start. Llanmadoc has a public house and a shop (for hot and cold drinks, ice-cream and so on), the latter owned by the local community. *Please take note of wildlife information and safety notices displayed along this route.*

START Car Park at SS 440935.

PUBLIC TRANSPORT Gower Explorer Bus Services 115 and 116 (usually with a change of buses at Cilibion or Llanrhidian Cross). Bus stop is at the village green.

I On reaching Llanmadoc village green (by car or bus), continue along the main street, passing another small green (with bench) on the left. At the junction by the church, take the right fork and descend the lane (the parking area is on the right, part way down). Continue down the lane, ignoring waymark signs leading to the right into Betty Church Nature Reserve. On reaching a group of houses, follow the lane round towards the left, looking out for a gate with National Trust signage, set back on the right.

2 Go through the gate, down the lane and then continue along the track. At a junction of tracks, continue AHEAD, below rock outcroppings on the left. At the next junction of tracks, turn RIGHT through a waymarked gate. Follow the sandy path that soon becomes a track and bends round to the right. Follow the track (please keep to the track as the area is used by ground-nesting birds – see signs alongside the track) to reach Whiteford Sands..

3 Follow the beach along towards Whiteford Point, near where the old iron lighthouse can be seen. *This should only be visited at LOW tide and care needs to be taken not to stay too long if doing so.* Continue to follow the beach around Whiteford Point, with dunes on the right. At the end of the dunes, bear HALF RIGHT towards the first group of conifers. Look for noticeboards just to the left of the conifers – one of these is a National Trust sign, adjacent to which a track runs into the trees.

4 Follow the main track through a succession of conifers, open dunes and broad-leaved trees. This area was used as an artillery range in the Second World War – please keep to the main track. Follow the track for about one mile. Ignore a kissing gate on the left and continue AHEAD to reach a gate across the track. Continue along the track and go through a second gate, after which the track runs along the boundary between the forestry and Cwm Ivy freshwater marsh. (A green-painted bungalow among the trees to the right is a holiday cottage that can be rented from the National Trust). At the far end of the forestry, go through a third gate and turn LEFT. Follow the outward route back to the car park/bus stop.

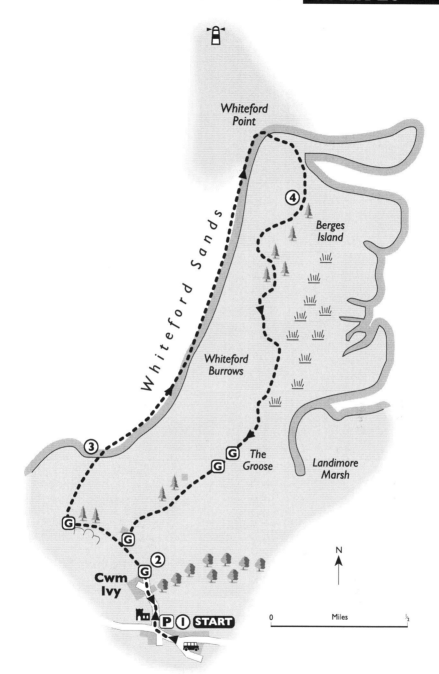

Whiteford
Point

Whiteford Sands

Berges
Island

Whiteford
Burrows

④

③

The
Groose

Landimore
Marsh

N

Cwm
Ivy

②

START

0   Miles   ½

LLANMADOC VILLAGE & NATURE RESERVES

DESCRIPTION A moderate 3½ mile walk, starting from Llanmadoc village. Descending the main street, the route then turns left on the Gower Way, following this through Frog Lane Nature Reserve. The next section of the walk heads through woodland, partly National Trust land and partly Betty Church and Cwm Ivy nature reserve. After a short section of lane and track, the route passes between forestry and freshwater marshland. A right turn leads to a path along a medieval sea wall between estuary and freshwater marshes. After another right turn, a footpath is followed back to Llanmadoc, ascending through woods and then crossing two fields to join an enclosed track. Allow about 2¼ hours for the walk.

START Car park at SS 440935.

PUBLIC TRANSPORT Gower Explorer Bus Services 115 and 116 (usually with a change of buses at Cilibion or Llanrhidian Cross). Bus stop is at the village green.

I From the car park head back up the lane, passing the church and a small green with a bench (both on the right). Pass a second small green on the right, by the bus stop (if arriving by bus join the walk at this point). Continue downhill on the main village street. Ignore the first footpath sign on the left and continue downhill to reach a second sign (not long after passing a house called 'Dane's Dyke', on the right). Turn LEFT on the side lane and follow this for a short distance to a gate on the right.

2 Go through the gate and follow the track downhill through woodland. Pass through a further gate and follow the track AHEAD to the right of a shed and then to the right of a house. Go through another gate and continue along the track, passing to the right of a cottage. Shortly after this, the track becomes a path that continues through woodland.

3 Ignore a set of steps on the left. After a few feet, turn LEFT through a kissing gate and follow the path along the lower edge of the wood. Part way along, pass through a second kissing gate that marks the boundary between National Trust property and the local nature reserve, Betty Church and Cwm Ivy Woods. Go through a third gate at the end of the wood and follow the track past an old building on the right. Head HALF LEFT up a drive to a lane.

4 Turn RIGHT on the lane and follow this past houses. When the lane bends round to the left, look for a gate with National Trust signage, set back on the right. Go through the gate and down the lane, which in due course becomes a track, to reach a waymarked junction. Go through the gate on the right and follow the track between forestry (on the left) and freshwater marshes (on the right). Pass through a gate and continue AHEAD to go through another gate.

5 Continue AHEAD on the track for about 100 yards, turn RIGHT and go through a kissing gate to follow the Gower Way along the top of a medieval sea wall separating Cwm Ivy freshwater marsh (on the right) from the estuary marsh on the left. At the end of the dyke, follow the path round to the left and go through a kissing gate. Ignore the other kissing gate on the right and continue AHEAD for a short way.

6 Go up the waymarked flight of steps on the right and cross a stile. Follow the path through the wood, ascending steps on the steeper sections, to a stile into a field. Head across the field to a stile in the far left corner. Continue along the left hand side of the next narrow field to a stile leading on to an enclosed track. Follow the track to a third stile, onto the road. Turn RIGHT and follow the road back to the bus stop/car park.

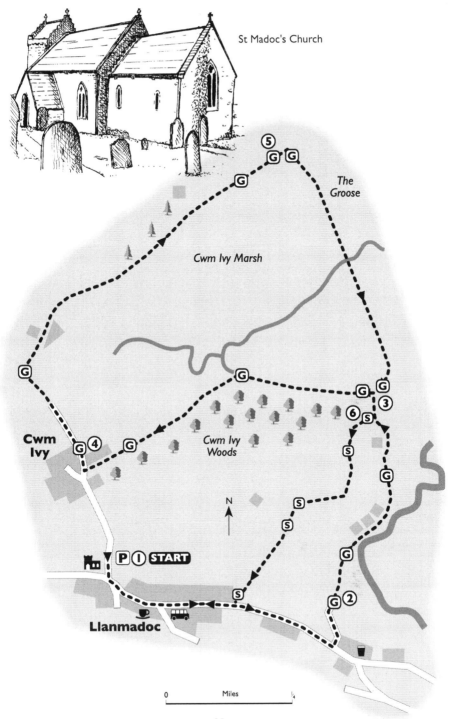

St Madoc's Church

The Groose

Cwm Ivy Marsh

Cwm Ivy

Cwm Ivy Woods

N

Llanmadoc

START

P (i)

0   Miles   ¼

WALK 25

LLANMADOC HILL

DESCRIPTION A moderate 3½ mile walk from Llanmadoc village up to the crest of Llanmadoc hill. Passing through the site of the Bulwark prehistoric hill fort, where several banks and ditches can be seen, the route follows the ridge along to the trig point near the far end, before descending to follow a lower level route back to the village. A wide range of excellent views can be seen on the way: over the tidal estuary to the Carmarthenshire and South Pembrokeshire coasts; the beaches and rocky tors of the coast line; Rhossili Down and Worm's Head; the farmlands of central Gower. Allow about 2¼ hours for the walk.

START Car Park at SS 440935.

PUBLIC TRANSPORT Gower Explorer Bus Services 115 and 116 (usually with a change of buses at Cilibion or Llanrhidian Cross). Bus stop is at the village green.

1 From the car park, head back into the village, passing the first green on the right, to reach the second green, where the bus stop is located (start the walk from here if arriving by bus). Follow the no-through lane leading from the back of the green (noticeboards indicate that this is the way to the village shop/café). Follow the lane past the shop and several houses, then round to the right, where the lane soon becomes a track.

2 Follow the track uphill through open and enclosed sections, remaining on the main track, to reach the open access hill land. Very soon after passing the gate to a house on the left, turn LEFT on a path that

leads through bracken. Follow this path for some way, with views over the estuary on the left, to reach the junction with a stony track. Houses can be seen ahead and lower down the hill at this point.

3 Turn RIGHT away from the stony track and follow a path that runs uphill through bracken. On nearing the crest of the hill, pass through one of the ditch and bank structures of the Bulwark and head HALF LEFT to join a grassy track that leads past a succession of hill fort ditches and banks. Continue to follow the track along the ridge, passing cairns off to the right. The track meanders towards the trig point, which is currently visible on the skyline ahead (the trig point passes out of view in due course, but it is easy to maintain direction until this is re-sighted).

4 From the trig point, there are views towards Rhossili Down and Worm's Head. When ready, follow the grassy track AHEAD and bear RIGHT on reaching a cairn on the right. Descend until passing a group of rocks on the right. Bear RIGHT on a grassy path that leads back along the hillside, allowing views of the estuary and Carmarthenshire coast beyond.

5 Eventually, come in sight of two houses on the left, at the edge of the open access land. Follow a path down towards the second house and turn RIGHT on a track. At a junction of tracks, bear LEFT and follow the outward track and then lane back to the village.

34

WALK 26
GELLI-HIR WOOD

DESCRIPTION Located on the edge of open access land at Fairwood Common, Gelli-hir Wood local nature reserve contains a mixture of broadleaved and wet woodland, some of which is ancient. Key features of the reserve are breeding birds (including buzzard, tawny owl and sparrowhawk); lower plants, fungi and invertebrates on fallen timber; moths and butterflies; dormice. There is also a bird hide, adjacent to a pool, on which mallard and moorhen can be seen, with the occasional green sandpiper. This is a generally easy route with about I mile walking within the reserve, for which about ¾ hour should be allowed – there are other paths in the reserve that walkers may wish to explore. This walk can be linked to Prior's Wood and Meadow, by following the road towards Cil-onen and then turning right on the Gower Way.
START Roadside lay-by at SS 562924.
PUBLIC TRANSPORT Gower Explorer 18 bus service crosses Fairwood Common. The nearest listed stop is at Cartersford, to the west of the road passing Gelli-hir, but the driver may be able to stop nearer to the turning, depending upon traffic.

1 Take the minor road leading north from the B4271, signposted for Cil-onen. Go over the cattlegrid and continue along the lane to the lay-by (on the left) and main reserve entrance (on the right). Follow the track into the reserve. Go through a gate and follow the path AHEAD for a short distance, then take the right fork. Follow the grassy track through the wood and then round to the left. Continue along the main path, crossing two small footbridges. Cross over a junction of paths and continue AHEAD to reach the junction with a wider track.

2 Turn RIGHT and follow the wider track, bearing left on this when it nears the edge of the wood. Keep to the main track and cross a further two small footbridges. At a junction with a wide track, turn RIGHT. Ignore paths leading off to the right and continue along the main track. At the next junction turn LEFT to reach the bird hide and pool.

3 When ready, start back along the outward route. Turn RIGHT at the first junction and then continue STRAIGHT AHEAD on the main track to return to the entrance to the reserve.

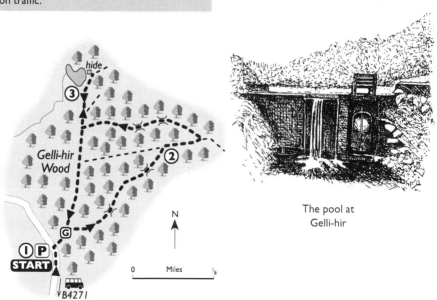

The pool at Gelli-hir

BURRY PILL & TOR GRO

DESCRIPTION This moderate 4¾ mile route passes through a range of contrasting scenery, starting with hill views, then descending through woodland to pass near a local church. The walk then follows an easy section of riverside, from which there is an optional extension to a hill top trig point with views. The next stage follows lanes to the village of Landimore, passing the National Trust Bovehill on the left. At the end of the lanes, a track is followed past another interesting contrast in scenery – woodland on the left and salt marsh grazing on the right, with a view ahead to Whiteford National Nature Reserve, with its dunes and small areas of conifer. Turning inland, the route leads up through woodland and across fields, passing near North Hill Farm before descending via enclosed track and lane to Cheriton and then back to Llanmadoc. Allow about 2¾ hours for the main route.

START Car Park at Llanmadoc village, SS 440935.

PUBLIC TRANSPORT Gower Explorer Bus Services 115 and 116 (usually with a change of buses at Cilibion or Llanrhidian Cross). Bus stop is at the village green.

From the car park, head back into the village, passing the first green on the right, to reach the second green, where the bus stop is located (start the walk from here if arriving by bus). Follow the no-through lane leading from the back of the green (noticeboards indicate that this is the way to the village shop/café). Follow the lane past the shop and several houses, then round to the right, where the lane soon becomes a track. Follow the track uphill through open and enclosed sections, remaining on the main track, to reach the open access hill land. Very soon after passing the gate to a house on the left, turn LEFT on a path that leads through bracken. Follow this path for some way, with views over the estuary on the left, to reach the junction with a stony track. Houses can

be seen ahead and lower down the hill at this point.

2 Turn LEFT and follow the stony track downhill. On nearing the junction with a road, turn LEFT and descend a grassy track towards a white house – look for the remains of an old gateway with possible house remains on the left. Cross the road and take the waymarked route between trees, just to the left of the house. Follow the old track down through the woods. On reaching a drive, follow this down to the road. Turn RIGHT and follow the road, soon reaching St Cadoc's Church, on the left (14thC, restored). An information board can be found just inside the churchyard gate and there are soft drink making facilities in the porch (plus a donation container!). When ready, continue a short way further along the road and take the waymarked footpath on the right.

3 Follow the driveway towards Bridge Pottery for a few yards, then cross the stile by the gate on the left. Head along the right hand side of the field to a second stile. Follow the path AHEAD through the wood, crossing a third stile and a section of boardwalk. At a two-way waymark post, take the right fork, soon leaving the woods. Head along the right hand side of two fields, connected by a stile. Pass through an open gateway into another field. Continue to follow the path along the right hand boundary, to reach a stile onto a bridleway (for an optional extension, turn RIGHT and follow the bridleway over an old bridge, up through the wood and round to the left to reach Ryer's Down. Head up to the trig point for views. Return to the main route when ready).

4 Cross the bridleway and the stile on the far side. Continue to follow the path along the right hand side of five fields, crossing six stiles on route. In a further field, head towards the house. Pass through a gate to the

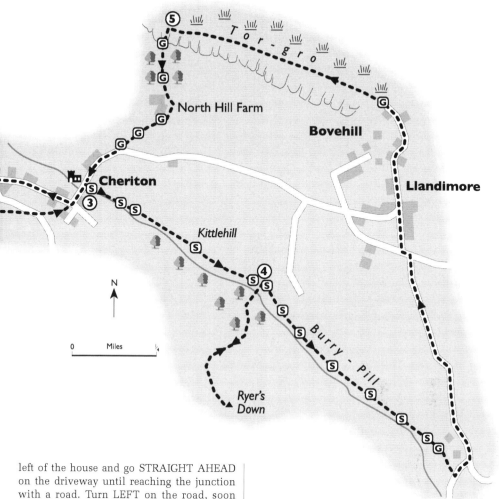

left of the house and go STRAIGHT AHEAD on the driveway until reaching the junction with a road. Turn LEFT on the road, soon taking the left fork at a junction. Follow the lane to the crossroads near Landimore. Cross the junction and follow the lane through Landimore. Keep to the lane, ignoring waymark signs to left and right. At the end of the lane, go through the gate ahead into Landimore Marsh. Keep to the track that runs ahead, below Tor Gro. After about 1 mile, at a waymark post, turn LEFT on a waymarked path into the wood.

5 Head up through the wood, climbing steeply at first and soon with a fence to the right. At the top of the wood, go through a kissing gate and follow the right hand side of the field. Pass a waymark post and continue to a waymarked gate on the right. Go through the gate and continue AHEAD to cross a track to the next waymark post. Pass to the right of the house and head for the left corner of the field. Go through a gate onto an enclosed track. Follow the track, passing through two more gates to reach the junction with a road. Turn RIGHT and follow the road down to Cheriton and then round to the right, back uphill to Llanmadoc.

1 From Llanrhidian Cross (by the bus stop), follow the road north into the village. Very soon, take the right fork and follow the lane down to the turning on the left for the church. Enter churchyard and head past the church to a stone stile in the far left corner of the churchyard. Follow the path through the lower edge of Llanrhidian Hill (National Trust) to the junction with a lane. Turn LEFT and follow the lane to the end. Continue AHEAD on the track. Branch HALF LEFT at a waymark sign. Follow the track to a stile and then along the left hand side of a field. Cross a further stile and continue to follow the left hand field boundary to an open gateway.

3 Go most of the way along the left hand boundary of the field, then go through a waymarked gate on the left. Follow the path round to the right. Go through a gate and follow the enclosed path AHEAD, being joined by a grassy track coming from the right. Pass an old building on the right and cross a track to a waymarked gate. Go through the gate and cross the left hand corner of the field to a waymark post for Weobley Castle. To visit the castle, go through the gate and head up the field (keeping to the left as in the safety notices) to the gate into the access route to the castle, which is a short way away to the left.

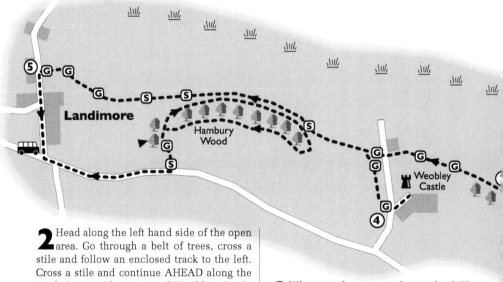

2 Head along the left hand side of the open area. Go through a belt of trees, cross a stile and follow an enclosed track to the left. Cross a stile and continue AHEAD along the track (now with a view of Weobley Castle on the hill ahead). Cross a stile and follow the path through the wood. Cross a further stile and continue on a path running half left up through the wood. At a three-way waymark post turn RIGHT through a gate (signed for Coast Path and Landimore). Continue STRAIGHT AHEAD to reach a gate into a field.

4 When ready, return down the hill to the Coast Path. Go back through the lower gate and turn SHARP LEFT. Follow the left hand boundary of the field to a waymarked stile on the left. Cross the stile and bear RIGHT. Follow the left hand side of a long field (Hambury Wood is now to the left, although there is no direct access from the Coast Path). Cross a stile and head across the field to a further stile. Bear HALF LEFT across the next two fields, passing through kissing gates on route. Follow the right hand side of a third field to a kissing gate onto a lane.

WALK 28

LLANRHIDIAN, WEOBLEY CASTLE & HAMBURY WOOD NATURE RESERVE

5 Turn LEFT on the lane and follow this to the junction. Turn LEFT again and follow the road, looking out for a stile on the left, just to the right of a stone wall on the left hand side of the road. Cross the stile and follow the field boundary to a gate into Hambury Wood Nature Reserve. Follow the circular path around the reserve and then return to the junction with the lane to Landimore village, from which a bus can be caught.

DESCRIPTION In total contrast with the beaches and soaring limestone cliffs of south and west Gower, the Coast Path runs between hilly woodland and salt marsh grazing land. There is the option of visiting the hill top remains of Weobley Castle on route (owned by National Trust and with an entrance charge). The final section of this linear walk uses a path in Hambury Wood Nature Reserve. Allow about 2¼ hours for this moderate 3¾ mile walk

PARKING Very limited in Llanrhidian, so suggest parking in either Crofty (SS 533957) or Penclawdd (SS 545959) and catching the bus, as below.

PUBLIC TRANSPORT Gower Explorer Bus Service 115 between Swansea and Llanmadoc passes the turnings for Llanrhidian and Landimore villages.

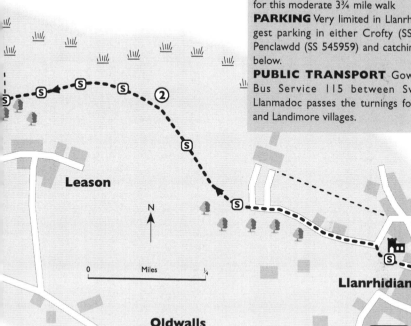

Leason

N

Oldwalls

Llanrhidian

START

0   Miles   ¼

PARC-LE-BREOS WOODS, BROAD POOL & GOWER WAY

DESCRIPTION A moderate 6½ mile walk following the Gower Way through woodlands at Parc-le-Breos and then along the boundary of fields and woods. On reaching Cilibion, there is a short roadside walk to Broad Pool Nature Reserve. Continuing along the unfenced road for a short way leads to a waymarked footpath that ascends the open access hill land to return to the Gower Way. The waymarked route and then a bridleway track are followed back to the start, passing a range of excellent hill views on route. Allow about 4 hours for the walk.

START Picnic area/small car park at SS 528887.

PUBLIC TRANSPORT Gower Explorer 118 stops near Penmaen church. Follow the lane to the right of the church for about ¼ mile. After crossing the cattle grid, look for the waymarked bridleway track leading half right and join the walk at this point*. The walk can be shortened by catching a bus to Swansea from the roadside near Cilibion (see stage **5** below and Gower Explorer timetables).

1 Face away from the picnic area and head RIGHT along the lane. On reaching a waymarked bridleway track on the left, turn onto this (*if arriving by bus, join the walk at this point*). At a junction of tracks, with a Gower Way plinth to the right, take the right fork. Follow the Gower Way along the base of the open access land to reach the point where it crosses a waymarked stile on the right.

2 Cross the stile and follow the path AHEAD, then turn RIGHT on a waymarked track. Follow the main track through the wood, ignoring side turnings, for about 1½ miles until reaching a junction of tracks, with a Gower Way plinth and waymark sign on the far side.

3 Turn LEFT and follow the track through woodland. At a junction, take the left fork (following the Gower Way waymark sign). Follow the track, which eventually becomes a path, and cross a stile out of woodland. Follow the right hand side of two fields, crossing a second stile on route.

4 Cross a third stile and follow a path through a short stretch of woodland to reach a stile on the left, with a Gower Way plinth on the right. Follow the right hand side of the next two fields, crossing a stile on route. Look for a Gower Way plinth on the right – at this point, turn RIGHT onto a track.

5 Cross a shallow stream and then cross two stiles on the left. Head along the left hand side of two fields, crossing a stile on route. Cross another stile onto a track and follow this AHEAD to the road*. Turn LEFT and follow the verge (with care – good visibility but fast traffic) to Broad Pool Nature Reserve.

6 When ready, continue along the road verge until reaching a waymark sign on the left. Turn LEFT on the footpath and follow this for about ¾ mile to a junction of paths near a field boundary on the left. Take the right fork and follow this uphill and gradually to the left, crossing over a junction with a straight track to reach the junction with the Gower Way, by a Gower Way plinth on the left.

7 Turn LEFT and follow the Gower Way to the point where this makes a sharp turn to the left. Continue AHEAD on the bridleway track to meet the junction with a lane. Turn either RIGHT to return to the parking area or continue AHEAD to the bus stop near the church at Penmaen.

* Buses to Swansea can be caught from here. The north and south Gower services connect at a small lay-by not far to the left of where the Gower Way meets the road.

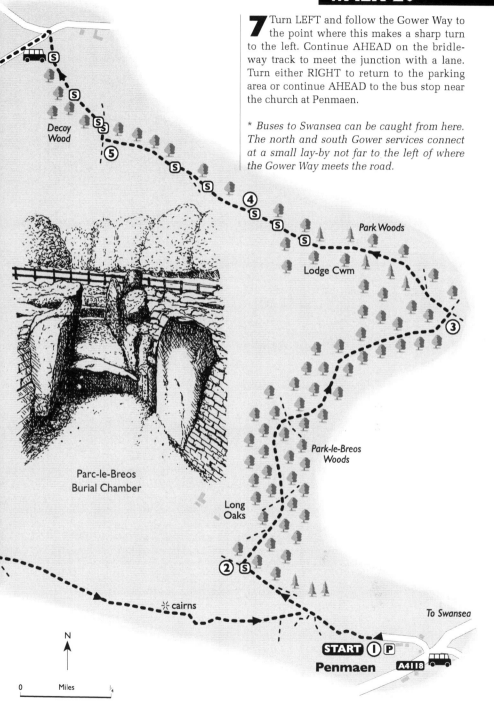

Decoy Wood

Park Woods

Lodge Cwm

Parc-le-Breos Burial Chamber

Park-le-Breos Woods

Long Oaks

cairns

To Swansea

START

Penmaen A4118

N

0 Miles ¼

WALK 30
PRIOR'S WOOD & MEADOW

DESCRIPTION Starting from Three Crosses, this walk leads by urban footpath and lane to a green area containing permissive footpaths. The key features of this area include woodland, wetland and a newly created large pond with two islands. From here, the route continues along the edge of Fairwood Common* to reach a stile into Prior's Wood and Meadow local nature reserve, where a circular path can be followed around the reserve. Key features of the reserve include secondary mixed broadleaved and wet woodland, lowland meadow, spinneys and hedgerow; shrub species, ground flora, ferns, bryophytes and lichens; meadow plants, grasses and sedges. This is a generally easy route of 2½ miles for which about 1½ hours should be allowed.

This walk can be linked to Gelli-hir Wood by following the road south along Fairwood Common and turning right at two junctions (this gives a view towards Swansea Airport and a chance that light aircraft may be seen in flight).

START Roadside parking in Three Crosses, near SS 567943.

PUBLIC TRANSPORT Bus service no 21 between Swansea and Three Crosses. Alight near the Country Stores.

Poundffald

Three Crosses

START

From the parking place/bus stop, head south, crossing a side road on the left hand side. A few yards beyond this, bear HALF LEFT on a tarmac footpath that soon becomes unsurfaced and leads past houses. On reaching Chapel Lane, cross over and follow the waymarked route down the lane opposite. Look out for a gate on the right, beyond which permissive footpath waymarking can be seen. Go through the gate and follow the left hand fork in the permissive route. Cross a small footbridge. On reaching a waymarked junction in the path, take the right hand fork that leads past a bench and round to the right. Pass to the left of the pond area, crossing two small footbridges. Turn RIGHT on nearing the trees. Before the end of the clearing, turn LEFT on a path into the trees and follow this round to the right to return to the lane.

2 Turn RIGHT and continue along the lane for a short way further, to reach a footpath sign on the right, leading to a gate onto Fairwood Common. Follow the path* along the left hand edge of the common. The stile is within trees and can be a little difficult to spot but is near the point at which the narrow band of trees edging the Common deepens into a wood.

3 Cross the stile and turn LEFT on the path through the reserve. Follow the path through the wood, to eventually reach a small footbridge. Cross this and turn RIGHT on the track, which crosses six walkway-style footbridges. Ignore the first exit style, to the left of a gate and head RIGHT on the path along the edge of the wood to complete the circular route at the entry point. Go back onto the Common and turn RIGHT to retrace the outward route. Follow the lane and footpath AHEAD to the bus stop/parking place**

*This section of the route can be very muddy following rain – it is best walked after dry weather.

**If you wish to walk to Gelli-hir Wood, the easiest way is retrace the outward route to Chapel Lane and turn LEFT. Turn LEFT again at the junction and follow the road south. Turn RIGHT at the next two junctions.

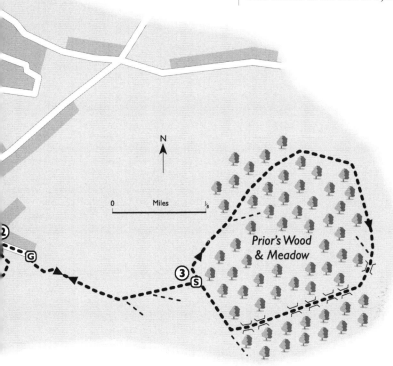

About the author, Jane Griffiths

Jane has enjoyed walking from an early age, exploring many parts of Wales and the West Country. Since the early 1980s she has lived mostly in mid Wales but also in Snowdonia for four years, where she was a mature student who took the opportunity for mountain walking. Having written four previous walking books, centred on mid Wales, exploring Gower in connection with this book has turned out to be both an adventure and a pleasure.

PRONUNCIATION

These basic points should help non-Welsh speakers

Welsh	English equivalent
c	always hard, as in cat
ch	as on the Scottish word loch
dd	as 'th' in then
f	as 'f' in of
ff	as 'ff' in off
g	always hard as in got
ll	no real equivalent. It is like 'th' in then, but with an 'L' sound added to it, giving 'thlan' for the pronunciation of the Welsh 'Llan'.

In Welsh the accent usually falls on the last-but-one syllable of a word.

KEY TO THE MAPS

- Main road
- Minor road
- Walk route and direction
- (1) Walk instruction
- - - - Path
- River/stream
- [G] Gate
- [S] Stile
- △ Summit
- Woods
- Pub
- (P) Parking

THE COUNTRYSIDE CODE

- Be safe – plan ahead and follow any signs
- Leave gates and property as you find them
- Protect plants and animals, and take your litter home
- Keep dogs under close control
- Consider other people

The CroW Act 2000, implemented throughout Wales in May 2005, introduced new legal rights of access for walkers to designated open country, predominantly mountain, moor, heath or down, plus all registered common land. This access can be subject to restrictions and closure for land management or safety reasons for up to 28 days a year.

Published by
Kittiwake
3 Glantwymyn Village Workshops, Glantwymyn,
Machynlleth, Montgomeryshire SY20 8LY

© Text & map research: Jane Griffiths 2011
© Maps & illustrations: Kittiwake 2011
Drawings:
Cover photos: *Main* – Three Cliffs Bay.
Inset – St Cennydd's, Llangennith. David Perrott

Printed by MWL, Pontypool.

ISBN: **978 1902302 88 1**